I SAW THE MOON WINK

AND OTHER POEMS

William A. Roberts

STOCKWELL
PUBLISHERS SINCE 1898

Published in 2022 by
William A. Roberts
East Malling, Kent
in association with
Arthur H Stockwell Ltd
West Wing Studios
Unit 166, The Mall
Luton, Bedfordshire
ahstockwell.co.uk

British Library Cataloguing-in-Publication Data
A catalogue record for this book is
available from the British Library.
ISBN: 9780722351659

Contents

Contents (cont.)

I Saw the Moon Wink

I Saw the Moon Wink

I've seen the strangest
thing:
last night,
I saw the moon wink.

I know it sounds silly,
but it's true.

It came out from
behind a big
old cloud…

just for a second…

winked…

and then went in again.

It just goes to show,
when you think
you're on your own,
there's always someone
to look out for you.

A Little Bit of Bread

I fed a duck
a little bit of bread,
filled it with lead shot
and now he's dead.

Then I fed the geese
and the swans too,
put in enough shot
to kill the likes of me and you.

You see, I'm not really wicked—
I love wildlife—
it's just that I've got
such a terrible wife.

She nags and she moans
all day long,
and killing a few birds…
well, I can't see the wrong.

It's not as if they are people,
or friends that I know.
I'm just practising…
for when I decide she must go.

Open the Curtains

Draw back the curtains,
open them wide,
let the sunlight
come inside.

Don't be mean.
Turn off the light,
throw back the curtains—
it's now daylight.

Come on, now—
don't be shy.
Daylight won't hurt you—
the sun's riding high in the sky.

Just grit your teeth
and grip them tight,
then throw open your arms
with all of your might.

There now—
isn't that fun?
Now we can both enjoy
the warmth of the sun.

A Crumpled Picture

The guns are singing
out their death song.
We're ready in our dugouts—
won't be long.

Every mouth dry
with anticipation and fear;
no loved ones to comfort you now…
no loved ones near.

For two hours these guns explode,
raining down death.
I look at the crumpled picture again
of you, my darling Beth.

Waiting at home,
fear in her heart,
now it's over the top
for the onslaught to start.

A thousand screaming men
race into no-man's-land,
hearts pounding faster,
rifles in hand.

The guns have stopped now;
the enemy are here.
My thoughts are on the Boche,
not you, my darling.

Slashing and tearing with bayonets,
kicking and biting too,
all for a few feet of land
and a crumpled picture of you.

Empty Goldfish Bowl

Our goldfish died
last night.

Found him floating
on top of the water
this morning.

Flushed him down
the toilet...

Looked at the bowl...
looks empty now,
without him.

Bit like this house...

looks empty without
you.

Saith the Lord

"This is My Son,"
saith the Lord,
whom I am very pleased with.

And oceans crashed ashore,
trees bowed
and flowers swayed,
and man bowed low.

This is My Son,
My only Son,
whom I shall sacrifice.

And the serpent
slid into the shadows
and whispered to man.

"Hear Me,
and behold your Saviour,"
said the Lord.

And the serpent
came out of the shadows,
and slid amongst man.

And man took our Saviour
and ridiculed Him,

They stripped Him
and beat Him
and forced a crown of thorns
upon His head.

And the serpent smiled.

And the Lord was saddened.

And man crucified
our Saviour
and left Him to die.

And the Lord turned away
and wept.

Going Home

I must go home—
it's that time of year.
I have no more money
and there's no more beer.

The tank's nearly empty
in my car
and still my journey home
is so very far.

I know she'll be waiting
by the fireside,
just like she did
as a new bride.

But the years have gone by
so very fast...
Here I am now—
home at last...

She's moved.

Prince Charming

I'm going to make you notice,
if it's the last thing I do.
I'll be your Prince Charming
with a glass shoe.

I'll whisk you away
to a fairy-tale land,
and life for us
will be oh, so grand.

I'm building up the courage,
day by day.
We pass each other in the mornings
and soon I will say...

"Hello."

Linen Basket

Linen basket's full—
should do some washing, really.
Can't be bothered—
should be all right for a day
or two.
Don't smell—
not like me.
Should wash—
still can't be bothered.
Life's like that
for me—
at the moment, that is.
Been that way ever since
the wife left

Closing My Eyes

I stand alone
in this world in which we live—
nothing to hope for,
nothing to give.

No friends have I
to rally around;
can't hear nothing—
not even the smallest of sound.

Depression for me
is a dangerous thing.
The razor in my hand
seems to sing.

So shiny and bright,
it slices my wrist.
This isn't a happy life—
there is no twist.

Just lie back in the bath,
now turning red,
closing my eyes…

Now I'm dead.

Her Name

I'm so in love,
yet all alone
I sit in this house,
so broken on my own.

Yesterday she left me
for another man,
saying he knows how to make her happy
the way only he can.

My heart is in pieces;
my eyes, they burn.
I have no one to confide in—
nowhere to turn.

Why has she left me?
I don't understand.
I never realised
that things had turned bland.

If only a second chance
I could have again,
I would wipe away
this terrible stain.

But she will never be mine
ever again,
and I have a lifetime to live
with this loss and this pain.

To wake each night
and call her name
over and over
and over again.

Don't Cry for Me

Don't cry for me, my darling.
I'm only off to war,
like so many thousands of men
who have gone before.

Don't cry for me, my angel,
for I will soon return
as one of the many heroes,
with more than enough love to burn.

Don't cry for me, my sweet,
as I lie dying in this field,
for I have your bloodstained photo
as my eternal shield.

Don't cry now, my darling,
for me in my unmarked grave.
Forget about me, your true love—
you have tears you now must save.

For when you read the letter
of how I gallantly died,
bury me deep in your heart
and wipe the tears you have cried.

Then start afresh, my sweetheart.
Start anew, my dove,
for I will always be with you,
watching from heaven above.

Nightmare

Midnight—
damp streets
that echo
with each
footfall.

Searching.

Heart beating
fast,
hand gripped
tight around
a knife.

Moonlight.

Flash of a
blade.

Muffled scream,
pain,
blood—
too much blood.

Footsteps running,
echoing;
heart pounding.

Sweating.

Wake up,
suddenly,
sheets tangled…

Only a dream.

Hospital

Sitting in the smoking room,
nothing much to do,
trying to avoid eye contact—
especially with you.

There's a hubbub of chatter
going on.
Look at the telly—
nothing really on.

Then a voice pipes up:
"Why do you always stare?'
"Because I'm from the starship *Enterprise*,"
I say without a care.

Slippers

You walked out and left me
a week ago,
when the land was frozen over
and covered in snow.

Didn't say a word
or leave a note.
It's been a week now, my darling,
and there's a lump in my throat.

You took your jewellery
and most of your clothes,
but you left me your slippers
that once covered your toes.

Tea in Berlin

Tanks are revving their engines—
we're ready to go.
We'll steamroll the Boche,
wherever we go.

Forwards to Berlin, boys—
that's the order of the day.
Then it's clutch down and gears home,
and then we're away.

Nothing can withstand us—
we're a sight to see.
We'll be in Berlin
just in time for tea

Death Unleashed

Death is ever present.
It surrounds me every day.
Death is my dear old friend…
who will never go away.

Down in the dugouts and trenches,
where the rats roam free,
Death is ever present,
always next to me.

And when the whistle blows
and we rush shouting over the top,
Death is in his element
and the killing never stops.

Only when the battle is over,
and the enemy are on the run,
does Death sit back and tell me
of all the fun he's had.

And as the night slowly settles
and machine guns are no more,
Death is finally quiet
and sleeps curled up on the floor.

War Games

Johnny's playing war games,
out amongst the rubble.
His dad is playing war games,
only he wears a stubble.

Johnny's gun is a piece of wood,
pretending to be real.
His daddy's gun is a real one,
and on his head he wears a hat of steel.

Johnny lays down and plays dead,
out amongst the rubble.
His father is lying in a field—
there's blood upon his stubble.

Flowers

I buy the wife
flowers every
week.

She puts them
in a vase,
feeds them water,
talks to them,
preens them…

And the bloody things
still die.

The Razor Looks Bright

Are those my eyes
that look back at me,
dead?

And that face,
pale
and drawn,
hair unkempt
and a week's growth
upon the chin
and cheeks?

Clothes dishevelled,
body unwashed,
dull…

Still,
the razor looks bright
against pale wrist.

Feeding Time… Tomorrow

Even the birds are
shivering.

That one on the left
is even shedding a
tear, I do believe.

Should go out
and feed them
a little bread
or hang those
peanuts up for
them to eat.

Fire's too warm though.

Looks cold out there,
all that snow…

I'll do it tomorrow…

if they're still there.

A Day at Ramsgate

Went down to see Dad.
Lives at Ramsgate,
tower block,
nice place,
nice view.

They've got a harbour there—
plenty of boats,
some big,
some small.

Said to Dad,
"How are you today?"

Without looking up from
the paper, replied,

"Your uncle's dead."

Affair

Her fingers were like
quicksilver
as she sliced the
carrots.

Faraway expression
in her eyes,

as if she were
someplace else.

Dreamy…

I know the affair
was over that evening,
when I found a tear
in my bowl of stew.

I Am What I Am

Love turned to
hate.
It's late
and long sinewy
tendrils are
creeping,
weeping,
winding,
binding
their way into
my mind.
I'm blind
to all that is
love.
I know only hate.
I am what I am:

MAN.

Rich in Mind

There's a house that stands
down our street,
where the kids run around
with nowt on their feet.

The widows need a clean
and the garden's a mess,
and it seems the little girl has
only one dress.

The wallpaper's hanging off
and the paint is peeling.
There's dirt on the floor
and there's dirt on the ceiling.

But give me this family
any time of year—
kids that don't swear
and have dirt in their ear.

Because they always say,
"Hello, mister",
from the oldest child,
right down to the little sister.

They have a gift
that many are without,
and they don't have to brag
or shout about it.

Manners, my friends,
don't cost a thing
and these poor children
now have everything.

Tomorrow

I see millions crying
a single tear;
I see a hundred people
stand and sneer.

I see a mother weeping
tears of joy
at the birth of
her unborn boy.

I see a father angered
by his wife.
I see him stab her
with a knife.

I see a man saddened
and full of pain
as they nail him down,
again and again.

I see a mother weeping
tears of sorrow
for her dead baby...
born tomorrow.

The Pump Is Purring

The pump is purring,
the fish are breathing,
the guinea pig is scratching;
now he's sneezing,

The dog's got fleas
and nibbles his leg.
The cat wants food
and starts to beg.

Kids are arguing,
breakfast everywhere.
Wash their faces—
I don't really care.

The wife's still out—
been gone all night.
When she gets home
she'll want to fight.

Bags are packed—
kids are ready too.
Leave a little note:
'Missing you.'

What I Hear

I hear the laughter
and the pain.
I hear the sadness
over and again.

I hear a child
clinging to its mother.
I hear the wind
calling something or other.

I hear the trees
as they bow down and cry.
I hear the stars falling
out of the sky.

I hear all of this
and much more
and remember our love
that we shared before.

Double Talk

She came in late
last night.
Asked her where
she'd been.

"Over my friend's,"
she replied.
Couldn't look at
me though—
kept shuffling
her feet.

She's not been
too well,
she stammered,
lipstick-smeared…

Then I noticed it
on her neck,
just in line with
her jumper.

Red in colour,
small
but distinct.

"Hope she gets
better soon,"
I added,
taking her coat
and hanging it up…

Heard her sigh.

Smiles of the Dead

Dead eyes
in a skeletal form
speak volumes at the suffering
these poor wretches have borne.

Huddled together,
scared of the light,
these poor creatures smile weakly
and muster the remainder of their might.

We rush forward
to help a swaying form,
bones sticking through
his uniform.

Gingerly we help them
to the waiting truck.
Thousands didn't make it,
but to these we are their good luck.

Tears burn my eyes,
at these skeletal forms,
smiling and laughing insanely
inside their uniforms.

I Don't Want to Be Alone Tonight

Nightmares,
black
and grey.

Listen to what I say.

I don't want to be alone tonight.

Feelings of insecurity,
feelings of doom—
these thoughts go through my head
while I sleep in this room.

Knives that stab,
slash
and cut.

Death surrounds me—
I feel it in my gut.

I don't want to be alone tonight.

When the night turns
black.

I don't want to be alone tonight.

While I lie upon my back,
feeling the cold,
clammy fingers of darkness
tightening around my mind.

Wake up sweating in the
early hours,
evil in my mind.

Only daylight defeats;
only daylight wins.
If only the daylight were here now,
I'd let it come in.

Take another sleeper—
maybe that will do
and the night will stay away…

If only that were true!

Argument

Eat my dirt,
eat my shorts.
You're a big ole boy—
you can eat all sorts.

Who am I to row?
It's her silly old…

No, I shan't call her names—
I love her too much.
It's not her fault
she's a little bit touched.

I know what I'll do:
I'll take her home.
Then you can argue
all on your own.

No Place Left to Run

From walking hand in hand slowly,
through a field,
to warplanes as a shield.

From chasing girls
just for fun,
to no place now
left to run.

From kissing lips,
soft,
warm
and light,
to wake up screaming
in the night.

How I Love You!

What is love?

Is love to be found
in a special look,
a caress,
kiss,
heartbeat?

Or the way I
tenderly,
lovingly
stab you
over
and
over again?

It Snowed Last Night

It's been snowing last
night.
Woke with a yawn,
threw back the curtains
and behold—
picture-postcard white,
everything looked pure.

Kids were out already,
throwing snowballs
at each other
or
pulling sledges.

I watched for a few
more minutes,
getting colder,
feeling colder,
then I turned
and went back
to bed.

Stop Phoning

Why are you always
moaning
and groaning
and phoning
me all the time?

Can't you see
that I don't love
you any more—
not like I did before
you started to drink
and run around with
other men!

Seems you now know
your mistake
and want me now.
For God's sake,
just leave me alone
and stop that incessant
phoning,
till four in the morning.

Don't you know
that you leave me cold—
as cold as ice?
Not very nice,
so let me be,
to get on with
my life.

Oh,
and by the way...
I'm going back
with my wife
and kids.

My Love for Her

She left me numb,
like flotsam on a
sea,
moss on a tree.
She hated me
with a passion.

Nothing was beyond
her hatred for me.

Yet I loved her—
cradled her,
as my hands
tightened around
her throat,
watched her face
bloat
then turn blue,
colour matching her
shoes.

When I Get Home

Call me
at a moment's notice—
don't hesitate
or faff around.

If you need a shoulder
to cry on,
I'll be there.

If you need cheering up,
I'm a call away.

If you need a little
DIY done,
then I'm your man.

No job too great;
no task too small.
Just call.

Failing that,
just tell me
when I get home
from work.

A Single Kiss

Why do women
fall in love?
Why do stars
shine high above?

Why do flowers
bloom in spring?
Why do girls like
a diamond ring?

Why does the sun shine
a golden yellow?
How does a single kiss
mellow…

the hardest of hearts?

My First Kiss

I'm lost in a dream.
My head's going around.
My eyes see nothing;
I hear no sound.

My sense of touch
is so enhanced.
It began when I felt courage
and took a chance.

It was that kiss
that you gave to me
that's making me behave
so strangely.

My Love

If you ever need a friend,
I will always be near,
to whisper sweet nothings
in your sweet ear.

If you ever need a friend,
just call out my name
and I will come running
time and again.

I will wipe away your tears
and make you smile.
I will walk an eternity for you,
or just a mile.

I will capture a star
so shining and bright
and lead you out of the darkness
and into the light.

I will do all of this
and so much more,
because I love you, my darling,
like I've never loved before.

Before the Tears Show

I don't believe you
when you say it's over,
that it's time for me
to move over

and let another man
take my place—
someone else
who will kiss your face.

I don't believe
we can't try again
to save our marriage,
to save me from pain.

So kiss me, my darling,
before you go.
Kiss me one more time
before the tears show.

The Same Game

As a boy,
I would watch
dogfights in
the sky,

each twist
and turn
captured by
my eye.

I would,
with heart
pounding
fast,

kill each
German,
right down
to the last.

But now I am
older
and my
memory
isn't the same.

I still look
towards the
sky,
and play that
same old game.

www.ingramcontent.com/pod-product-compliance
Lightning Source LLC
Chambersburg PA
CBHW031530040426

42445CB00009B/465